BRITAIN IN OLD PHOTOGRAPHS

PORTSMOUTH
& SOUTHSEA

PETER ROGERS

SUTTON PUBLISHING LIMITED

Sutton Publishing Limited
Phoenix Mill · Thrupp · Stroud
Gloucestershire · GL5 2BU

First published 1996

Cover photographs: *front*: the entrance to HM
Gunwharf; *back*: the new South Parade Pier.

British Library Cataloguing in Publication Data
A catalogue record for this book is available from the
British Library.

ISBN 0-7509-1296-0

Typeset in 10/12 Perpetua.
Typesetting and origination by
Sutton Publishing Limited.
Printed in Great Britain by
Ebenezer Baylis, Worcester.

CONTENTS

Camber Docks. This location provides evidence of man's earliest activities on Portsea Island. Archaeological excavations carried out on the adjacent shoreline show that our ancestors had visited, and later settled the site, from the Neolithic to the Bronze Age and beyond.

INTRODUCTION

Whatever justification there may be for the claim that Portsmouth is the only city in the world to totally occupy an island location, the distinction can, and does, apply to Portsmouth's unique position within the United Kingdom. When achieving the status of a city in 1926, the town had already extended its boundaries to the mainland and included Cosham, Wymering and Paulsgrove as early as 1920. The limits of the city were further extended in April 1932 when Drayton, Farlington and parts of Portchester were also absorbed within the growing metropolis.

With the exception of a number of aerial views of Cosham and the Portsdown, the pictorial content of this volume will be principally confined to the Island of Portsea (Portsmouth and Southsea) and will include few, if any, items which have appeared in previous works of this nature.

The reader may well question the occasional use of photographs which, of no great age or antiquity, are included in a publication of old photographs. The answer is of course that Portsmouth, heavily blitzed during the Second World War, has necessarily suffered a considerable number of changes in the geography of its street patterns and buildings. Vintage pictures of the 1950s, '60s and '70s are included to illustrate the removal of the last of the bomb damage, as well as the neglected areas of the city, and to highlight the growth and development of the new Portsmouth.

Town planning, while not to everyone's satisfaction, has included the rebuilt Guildhall, its square, public library, civic offices, docklands (including the new Continental ferry port), university expansion and many examples of domestic housing and modern shopping. Coupled with this is the fact that Portsmouth still remains the most densely occupied city in Great Britain.

What is the yardstick by which we measure history and the passage of time? As an example, it may be suggested that the first of the pictorial histories relating to Portsmouth, which appeared in 1975, made use of photographic examples from the turn of the century to the 1930s. We are now rapidly being overtaken by technology as it is applied to town planning, building methods and styles; so much so, that it is becoming increasingly difficult to comprehend and recall, say, the city of 1975, let alone 1930. Topographical scenes depicting early delivery vehicles, tramcars and horses all serve to remind us that the 'passing scene' is indeed passing from our memories. One of the many interpretations of history is that 'History is a thing of the past'. Do not then lose sight of the fact that the past is as recent as yesterday!

Interest in the publication of old photographs was originally stimulated locally with the successful launch of *Portsmouth Old and New* by David Francis, E.P. Publishing Ltd, 1975. Since that date, David Francis and Peter Rogers have together, and individually, compiled, and had published, several other volumes of a similar nature. Each time they have drawn on the wealth of interesting old photographs which exist in personal collections and local archives, as well as on their own extensive knowledge of the history of Portsmouth and its environs.

Nationwide, and indeed worldwide, interest in the nostalgia generated from the study of vintage photographs has created a demand and a ready market for books devoted to the subject. An invitation to compile and produce yet another pictorial history of Portsmouth and Southsea for Sutton Publishing was a challenge readily accepted. The author's involvement with a previous title, *Portsmouth in Old Photographs*, Sutton Publishing, 1989, and its subsequent successful marketing and sale, was all the assurance needed to commence the collection and research for a follow-up edition.

The city of Portsmouth has justifiably always been conscious of its rightful place in the history of the nation; this awareness has resulted, over many years, in the official publication of definitive volumes and learned papers on the subject. In addition to these works of a civil and academic standard, there have been many worthy contributions from individual authors and our local centres of learning. Pictorial history books which draw on vintage photographs for much of their content have also established a place and a need among a public anxious to learn more about the origins of their city. Photographs provide that *aide-mémoire* to our older citizens and assist younger members of the population in relating to present-day conditions, locations and situations.

This new volume will undoubtedly prove to be a worthy successor to the earlier title and, containing a plethora of material as yet unpublished, should have an immediate appeal to students and devotees of local history.

In conclusion, it may be suggested that writers and compilers of pictorial histories have reached the archival limits of old photographs and that the source and supply must, at some time, come to an end. Don't you believe it – photographs taken today are certain of a place in tomorrow's history books!

Nostalgia, after all, is said to be a thing of the past.

PORTSMOUTH,
A BIRD'S EYE VIEW

Wartime bombing of the High Street resulted in the destruction and subsequent removal of buildings previously fronting the Anglican Cathedral Church of St Thomas. The cathedral is in the adjoining St Thomas's Street and, until the clearance of the bombed and damaged properties, was not generally visible from the High Street.

Ravelin House is seen against a backdrop of postwar high-rise buildings, Portsdown Hill and the dockyard. Now part of the University of Portsmouth, the house was so named because of its proximity to the East Ravelin of the town's ancient defences. It was the home of Field Marshal Montgomery during the period when he was senior military commander at Portsmouth.

Photographed in August 1978, Portsmouth harbour railway station and jetty are seen with a British Rail Isle of Wight ferry at its berth. In the immediate foreground, Sealink car ferries are at their moorings. Looking shorewards, the coach and bus transport interchange is under construction with the Portsea Hard and small craft to the left and HM Gunwharf, with its military landing craft, to the right.

The hub of town centre shopping is shown here – a precinct in Commercial Road, crossing from right to left. The lower left hand corner shows the roof parking areas beneath which is the controversial 'Tricorn' shopping complex. Charlotte Street and Moores Square market indicate that the scene was recorded on a Friday or Saturday. The Cascades Shopping Centre has yet to be built.

Central Southsea, photographed from approximately 1,000 ft during the summer of 1968. Victoria Road South crosses from left to right, with Marmion Road cleaving its way towards St Jude's Church and Palmerston Road precinct. A number of significant changes have taken place in the ensuing years; the Methodist church on the corner of Hamilton Road has given way to modern housing, and land clearance in Marmion Road is in preparation for a planned Waitrose store and multi-storey car park.

The intended reclamation of Milton Locks and the construction of a marina at Eastney Lake never did take place. From 1966, however, the shoreline was cleared of its resident houseboats and the local High Street of the chalets and bungalows. For several generations, these served as weekend and holiday homes for those fishing and sailing folk who enjoyed escaping the town and its bustle for the quiet of the Milton shore.

Eastney peninsular together with the narrow channel of Langstone harbour entrance. The almost unique eighteenth-century star-shaped Fort Cumberland dominates the upper landmass.

The peninsular, seen for a second time, is little more than an ancient sand-bar reaching to the ferry point and, at the same time, forming a protective barrier almost encircling Eastney Lake.

The future of the city airport was the subject of much speculation following its closure in 1973. Suggestions included the relocation of Pompey Football Club from its present home at Fratton Park; looking north with Langstone harbour on the right, it appears to be the ideal situation for such a move with easy access from road, rail and motorway.

The airport is now seen, top, with Ports-creek on the left of the picture. The trees conceal the remains of the massive line of fortifications which once defended Portsmouth's northern shores.

Albert Johnson quay at Rudmore became a necessary addition to the city's docking facilities when it was opened for business in February 1968. The Camber docks had long been overtaken by the increased amount of shipping wishing to use the facility – the shoreline at Rudmore provided the obvious solution for expansion.

The Albert Johnson quay, an important location, prime for development. With the Royal dockyard on the left and Whale Island on the right, a small harbour is formed within the Portsmouth harbour itself.

Portsmouth's Continental ferry port now dwarfs the earlier Albert Johnson quay. The reader will hardly fail to notice the establishment of a complex system of docks and warehouse facilities together with the disappearance of the gas holder and the burial ground, which now lies beneath the pale-coloured car and lorry park, seen lower centre.

This wider view of the proposed docklands reveals the street pattern prior to the major redevelopment of Rudmore. The burial ground of 3½ acres is seen denuded of the many hundreds of memorial headstones which had been its Victorian legacy.

A heavy summer heat haze mars the quality of this aerial view of Portsea Island, although almost every feature of the landscape is easily recognizable.

Ports-creek, the narrow waterway dividing Portsea Island from mainland Cosham would, in ancient times, be crossed at one or more fording places accessible only at low water. The first of the bridges known to have spanned the creek was sited at a point where Tudor Crescent is now situated. A line drawn between the two white crosses, upper left and lower right, indicates the old road through Cosham to the bridge and the Portsmouth shore.

Crookhorn and Farlington, showing the 1970 development of housing, schools, a major road cutting through the hill and the planned new municipal golf course.

Further development on Portsdown Hill, this time at the George Inn crossroads in 1968. Thousands of tons of chalk were excavated to create a flyover and so improve an inadequate road system. The George now occupies an island site.

Aerial photograph of Farlington and the western edge of Bedhampton, May 1963, recorded at 10,000 ft. In appearance, the landscape is perfectly flat; in reality, you are looking at the eastern end of the Portsdown with the hill slopes running away in each direction. The white scar is all that remains of the Farlington Redoubt while, to its left, is the unique shield-shaped copse known locally as 'Dead Man's Wood', alongside the tortuous route of the original Crookhorn Lane. Top left of the picture is Morelands anti-aircraft site with its huts and gun pits still in evidence.

Wymering manor house amid the trees, just right of centre. The building occupies a site both Roman and Saxon in origin and has a documentary history pre-dating the Domesday Survey of 1086. The photograph was taken in 1946 following wartime occupation by the army.

The old manor house, can now be identified on an island site surrounded by private housing. Gone are the numerous trees which had previously ensured a rural setting, leaving both the building and its near neighbour, the Church of SS Peter and Paul, exposed to full public view.

PORTSMOUTH
POT POURRI

Portsmouth & Southsea railway station, 1876, the year in which the main line was extended to Portsmouth harbour; the overhead platform and canopy confirm the date. The building of dark red Portsmouth bricks and stucco dressings was once described as being in a style of the French Renaissance.

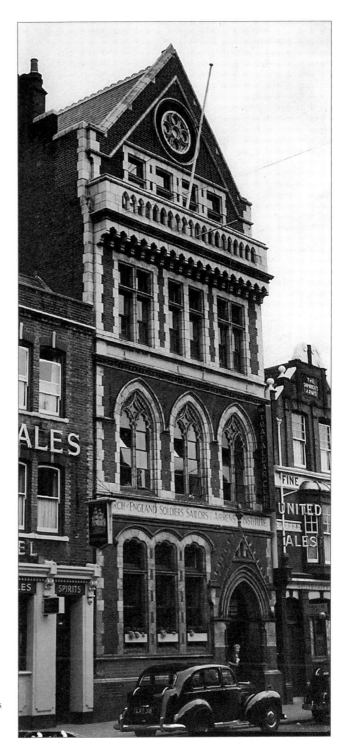

Generations of servicemen have referred to this building as 'The Traf', it being the Church of England Soldiers, Sailors and Airmens Institute, the Trafalgar Club, in Edinburgh Road. Opened in December 1906, it still provides accommodation today as a hall of residence for university students.

The Trafalgar building conceals a secret known only to a handful of Portsmouth folk. Measuring an impressive 8 ft by 30 ft and painted in full colour, this mural by Portsmouth-born artist Eric Rimmington is one of a number of his works gracing the walls of buildings within the city. Employing artistic licence, the painter has created a blend of Portsmouth old and new, using his local knowledge to introduce buildings and features of earlier centuries into the city of the 1940s, all viewed from the vantage point of the main railway station. Painted in about 1946, the work has been the subject of recent restoration.

On 10 January 1941 disaster struck at the Guildhall when several showers of enemy incendiary and one high explosive bomb totally destroyed the interior of the building. Rebuilding commenced in April 1955 and was completed by August 1958, when the various administrative departments of the city were reinstated.

The second phase of creating a new city centre involved sweeping away those premises which had previously faced the Guildhall and replacing them with the massive complex now housing the civic offices, as seen in this view recorded in June 1974. On completion, attention was then focused on developing the impressive multi-functional Guildhall Square, the 'plaza' of the previous picture.

The rebuilding of the city centre has been achieved and includes the law courts (bottom left) central library, civic offices and the several blocks of commercial business premises seen in the picture.

This postcard, *c.* 1905, portrays the town hall and square in the years before the motor vehicle dominated such topographical views. The electric tramcar had only recently been introduced to our streets (1901), and at this time horse-drawn transport still held sway.

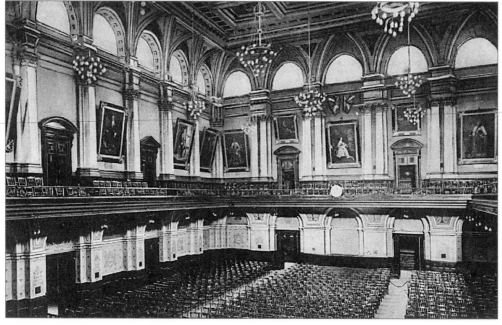

The magnificence of the Guildhall concert hall, 1908. With seating for 1,800 people, and heavily decorated with portraits of Their Majesties, it was undoubtedly the show-piece of the city until its destruction in the Second World War.

25 PORTSMOUTH. — Victoria Park and
Roman Catholic Cathedral. — LL.

Until 24 April 1878, when Victoria Park was opened, Southsea Common had been the only area of public recreation on Portsea Island. Thanks to the determined efforts of several local councillors, a section of land was negotiated for and released by the War Office for use as a 'Peoples' Park'.

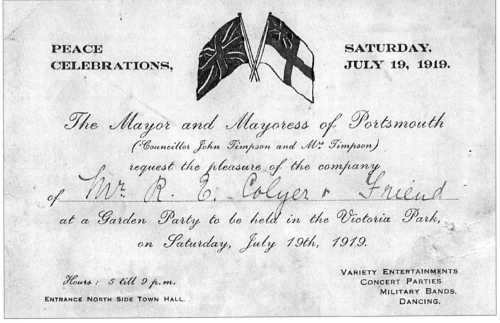

While the armistice had been declared in November 1918, peace was not ratified until 19 July 1919. Celebrations were held nationwide and Portsmouth contributed to the fun in several ways, one of them being a garden party to be attended by honoured guests in Victoria Park.

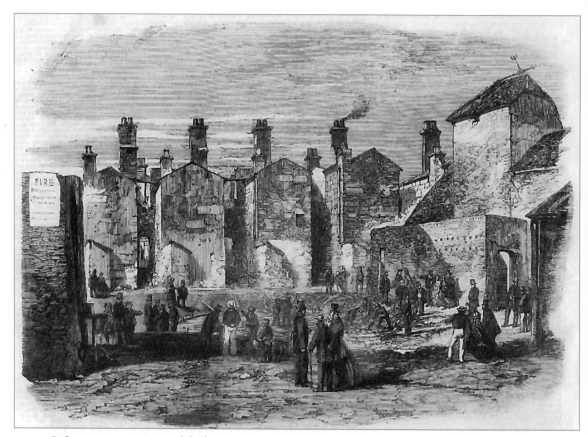

Reference to newspapers of the last century reveal that fires within the town were fairly commonplace; not surprising, in fact, when we consider construction methods and materials used in many of the older properties. A particularly disastrous example was this reported incident at the rear of Commercial Road in March 1861 when a circus owned by Messrs Cooke was completely destroyed. One elephant, one camel and eight of the most valuable horses were killed. Thirty-seven horses were saved although all of the circus materials were lost. Six houses in adjoining Buckingham Street were also destroyed and a further eight severely damaged.

A fire of greater significance, this time involving the loss of human life, was to strike the family and business of Harry Harrison in April 1912. Established as a naval and gentlemen's outfitters at No. 96 Queen Street in Portsea, the family consisted of Flora and Harry Harrison, Celia aged 6 years, Phillip aged 4 years, Sarah aged 2 years and an infant son Cecil aged 4 months; a live-in maid servant, Ellen Mason, aged 16 years, completed the household. The fire, on 16 April, completely destroyed the property and claimed the lives of Flora, Sarah, Phillip and Ellen. Harry Harrison escaped with the baby by climbing along an outside coping; Celia was rescued by the police. The picture shows a part family group outside the premises in 1908.

The following eight photographs were taken a mere twenty-three years after the tragic Queen Street fire. Together, they give an insight into the crowded conditions of Portsea and Landport's narrow streets — later to be demolished under the slum clearance act of the 1930s or by Hitler's bombs in the Second World War. This first view is of Havant Street.

Cross Street, Portsea, which connected Queen Street with Orange Street.

Blossom Alley. On the morning of Saturday 23 January 1923 the alley achieved particular notoriety when prostitute Mary Pelham was found murdered at No. 14. Her murderer was never found, nor was a motive established. The tragedy did, however, bring the squalid state of the slums of Portsea to the attention of the public and the authorities.

College Street, Portsea.

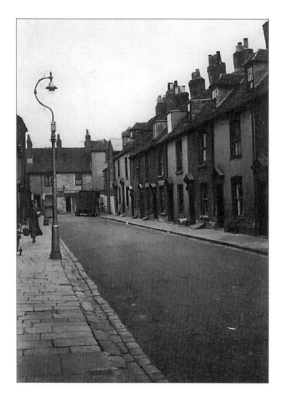

Orange Street, Portsea.

Landport View, Landport. The bunting is
displayed for the Silver Jubilee of their majesties
King George V and Queen Mary in 1935.

Chelsea Place, Landport. The modern Cascades
Shopping Centre covers this area today.

Town Street, Landport.

Workhouses for the destitute poor existed in both Portsmouth and Portsea; the two establishments were reluctantly combined in 1836. A site was later obtained for new premises in St Mary's Road which opened in 1845. It was to be another thirty-six years before the building pictured here was dedicated for the sole use of vagrants in 1881. Known as the casual wards, accommodating visitors, distinct and separate entrances were provided for both men and women.

Malthouse Road, Buckland, August 1974. During the years of postwar planning, sights such as this were commonplace in the town. Row after row of Victorian terraced houses were sacrificed in order to create the Utopian pipedream of twentieth-century architects. Novel though the new estates may be, with properties boasting every 'mod con', there are many who were reluctant to leave what had perhaps been the family home for several generations.

Lake Road has also had to suffer the inglorious attentions of the planner's zeal. In its day the road had contributed to the city's business and commercial interests, its shops providing a great variety of goods and merchandise. As Lake Lane, its early nineteenth-century origins can be traced in these old cottages which were later converted into shops in order to compete with their business neighbours.

Entertainment was also provided in Lake Road with two theatres, the Prince's and the Palladium. To counter the opposition from picture palaces in the 1930s, they both subsequently became cinemas themselves. The Prince's was destroyed by enemy action during the Second World War; the Palladium ended its life as a warehouse for a commercial clothier before its demolition in 1980.

Another form of entertainment has been provided in Portsmouth since the introduction of professional football in the late nineteenth century. On 13 September 1913 Pompey played Coventry City in a Southern League Division One match. The crowd of 12,000 witnessed a scoreless draw. A fashion note of the day is that every spectator is wearing a hat.

Football clubs now include many ladies among their fans, who attend matches as devoted supporters. In the early years of the century, however, it was probably thought to be 'not the done thing' and the appearance of a lady at Fratton Park was a rarity!

Although Portsmouth has been the home of the Royal Navy for several hundred years, it has, perhaps more importantly, been a garrison town. In the latter half of the nineteenth century there were nine barracks on Portsea Island housing both military and Royal Marines. The principal museum of the city is now housed in this classically styled barracks, a permanent reminder of the city's military importance.

Great Salterns House overlooks Langstone harbour from its vantage point on the Eastern Road. Owned by the city it is now used primarily as golf club premises. No confirmed date for its construction is known, although a map dated 1716 appears to show such a property at the harbour's edge on land which is marked 'Lady Carrington's'. Lewis's map of 1833 shows the house positioned as we know it today.

A redundant Isle of Wight paddle-steamer, probably the *Sandown*, beached on the Paulsgrove shore behind Bert's transport café in the 1960s. The café proprietors were quick to notice its advertising potential alongside a busy road. A city sandwiched between two harbours is almost certain to receive as an unwanted legacy the remains of old and abandoned shipping and small craft. Derelicts of many types have habitually littered our coastal harbours and inlets and, although the examples shown in these two photographs have been removed, there are always more seeking a final resting place!

The shoreline at Milton Locks, 1958. Although these old vessels and houseboats were removed, others have somehow been introduced to take their place.

PORTSMOUTH,
THE OLD TOWN

Possibly Portsmouth's most popular and historic landmark is the Round Tower which has commanded the harbour entrance since about 1417. Originally, together with a companion on the Gosport side of the harbour, it was constructed to protect the town from attacks by the French who had made periodic raids when they both sacked and fired the small community.

An engraving of about 1840 includes the Round Tower while looking across the harbour mouth to Gosport. A massive chain, part of the defences, was to be drawn up from its position on the sea bed to prevent enemy vessels from gaining access to the harbour.

5 *PORTSMOUTH* — *The Saluting Battery.* — *LL.*

The defensive position immediately to the east of the Round Tower was part of Point Battery. Displaying no modesty, local boys are seen skinny dipping from the steps of the Sally Port.

„Sallyport" Portsmouth.

Sally Port at high water, traditionally the departure point of our many sailor heroes.

Old Sally Port, Portsmouth.

An exposed beach at low water looking east from the Sally Port, shows the continuing line of the defensive wall, Victoria Pier and the Square Tower. This tower, the town's second major defence work, was constructed in about 1494.

The Gosport shore with HMS *St Vincent* at its moorings, *c.* 1880, can be seen beyond the Saluting Battery and the Square Tower. The battery was the traditional site from where salutes were fired for visiting royalty.

The Battery platform also doubled as a grandstand for those spectators watching the military church parades each Sunday. The garrison church and parade ground are sited to the right of the picture.

Hurricane force winds together with high tides wrought havoc along Britain's south coast in October 1987. Portsmouth's centuries-old defensive walls, having faced the elements since at least the sixteenth century, were finally breached, not by an enemy but by nature itself. The wall seen here fronts the Saluting Battery pictured in the previous two photographs.

Royal and traditional salutes are now fired from Blockhouse Fort in Gosport (there is no longer a military presence in Portsmouth). Before the practice ceased in Portsmouth, the location had been moved from the old Saluting Battery site to this position overlooking the garrison church on the one side and Long Curtain moat on the other. The tradition of firing an evening gun at sunset each day (see picture) finally ceased in September 1931.

The final battery of saluting guns was located along the bank overlooking the Long Curtain moat and the sea – an ideal situation for welcoming visiting dignitaries before they entered the harbour.

Pembroke Road, Old Portsmouth, *c.* 1895. Remove from the picture the Wesleyan chapel and White's Dining Rooms and the view is almost unchanged today.

St Thomas's Anglican Cathedral is seen beyond the cleared bomb site in the High Street. Old Portsmouth suffered badly from the bombing and it is more than surprising that the cathedral escaped with little damage. Buildings standing in front of the cathedral had been destroyed, as were properties in St Thomas's Street at the rear.

Quebec House in Bath Square was built in 1754 by public subscription, as a bathing house. With a weatherboard construction, it is unique in Portsmouth.

Constructed between 1858 and 1865, partially on the site of the old Georgian Theatre Royal, the Cambridge Barracks were designed by architects sympathetic to the Georgian influence of the High Street. The much later departure of the military left the building vacant at a time when the Portsmouth Grammar School was seeking to expand. The facilities and location proved to be most suitable – and the school took possession in 1926.

PORTSMOUTH HARBOUR SCENES

A treasured engraving of Portsmouth harbour dated 1885, from a painting by C. Napier Hemy. The two 'old salts' are making the craft shipshape while sailing home after a fishing trip at sea. The man-of-war is almost certainly HMS *Victory*, which occupied a permanent berth off the Gosport shore at this time.

A photographic view complements the previous engraving; it is still looking towards the harbour entrance. Both pictures are of the same vintage.

The harbour has always been busy and full of shipping, both this century and during the last. This photograph was taken in about 1885 and shows that at this time there appears to be little enough room for free passage. On the left is the line of old hulks known as 'Rotten Row' – either redundant Royal Navy vessels or perhaps the last of the French prizes; many served out their time as prison ships before being broken up.

Following years of active service, HMS *Victory* was allowed to spend her retirement moored in Portsmouth harbour. In 1903 the old vessel was almost sunk at her moorings when the obsolete battleship *Neptune* broke away from its tow-line while leaving harbour. After considerable repairs, serious thought was given to the future safety of the Trafalgar veteran but it was not until 1922 that she was given a permanent home, a dry dock in Portsmouth dockyard.

Little or no money was available from the Admiralty to save *Victory* so an appeal was launched and directed by the Society for Nautical Research. Large sums were raised for both the docking and restoration and the ship finally entered the oldest dry dock in the dockyard on 12 January 1922. She remains today, a symbol of both the Royal Navy and the city of Portsmouth.

A postcard dated 1911 features the harbour with HMS *Martin* occupying centre stage. *Martin*, a sailing brig, was tender to HMS *St Vincent*, the redundant man-of-war which, berthed near the entrance to Haslar Creek, served as a boys' training ship. Sharing the scene is HMS *Victory* together with a number of steam-driven Royal Navy vessels.

Foudroyant, formerly the frigate HMS *Trincomalee*, was the oldest British warship afloat until July 1987, when she was transported 'piggyback-style' to Hartlepool for a major refit. A familiar sight in Portsmouth harbour, she provided sea training for generations of children and teenagers. Memorable holidays were spent by young people in an atmosphere reminiscent of Nelson's day. Following her extensive refit, the ship is destined to remain at Hartlepool.

Rarely seen paintings by the Gosport artist Martin Snape. This painting, dated 1911, is titled *Gosport from Old Portsmouth*.

This second of the Snape paintings is dated 1912 and titled *Entrance to Portsmouth Harbour*.

HMS *Zephyr*, July 1907, is seen leaving harbour at considerable speed, which seems foolhardy bearing in mind that a similar vessel, HMS *Coquette*, had rammed the dockyard coaling depot at speed just three months earlier.

The use of barrage balloons to deter enemy aircraft during raids on Portsmouth is well known. They were also used at sea to defend convoys and, in this case, to protect harbour shipping.

HMS *Dolphin*, the Navy's shore-based submarine depot at Gosport, was closed and transferred to another location in 1996. These vessels, familiar to the harbour scene since 1904, will now only favour us with an occasional visit. Submarine A3 is viewed while passing HMS *Victory*, 1904.

Heroes all, submariners risked their lives each time they went to sea; the early experimental years took their toll with frequent mishaps and tragedies. An explosion on board A5 in February 1905 took the lives of a lieutenant and five crew members. Later, in February 1912, fourteen officers and men lost their lives when A3 was sunk in collision with HMS *Hazard* off the Isle of Wight.

Moored in the upper reaches of the harbour at Portchester Creek, HMS *Vernon*, in company with several other old hulks, became the Navy's torpedo and wireless telegraphy school. The unlikely collection of old vessels remained as such, until the re-location of the school to a shore base at HM Gunwharf in 1923. As an independent establishment, *Vernon* closed in March 1986.

At Hardway, on the Gosport side of the harbour, was yet another group of old vessels, known collectively as HMS *Fisgard*. A training school for apprentice boy artificers, the several vessels were changed from time to time, but at the closure of the establishment in December 1931 they were *Spartiate, Terrible, Hindustan* and *Sultan. Sultan* spent her remaining years in Portsmouth dockyard, while her companions were sent to be broken up.

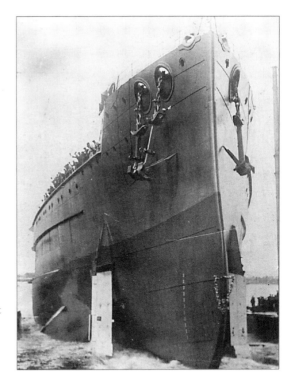

The building and launch of HMS *Andromeda* in 1968 brought centuries of ship building at Portsmouth to an end. The premier naval port had also been Britain's principal yard for the construction of naval vessels. Launched by the Countess of Beauchamp in September 1908, HMS *St Vincent* is pictured entering the water.

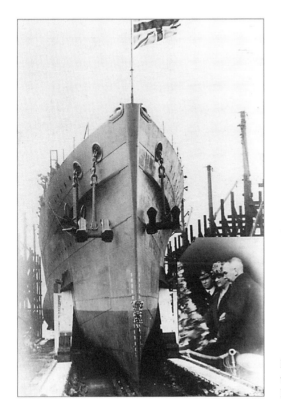

HMS *Suffolk*, the first of our postwar cruisers, was despatched by the Marchioness of Bristol, 16 February 1926.

Built by Harland and Wolff, this mammoth floating dock arrived in Portsmouth Harbour on 2 August 1912 and remained until 1939 when it was towed to the then naval harbour at Malta. Unique in construction, docks such as this provided dry docking facilities where none other was available. A succession of such 'craft' have been based at Portsmouth, though the last was scrapped in 1954.

The 1912 dock was very soon put to the test with HMS *Monarch*; *Monarch* was of the 'Orion' class and weighed in at about 22,500 tons.

Royal yachts were frequent visitors to the harbour; each of our naval reviews has been attended by a reigning British monarch and often by visiting royalty. Pictured here is the second of Queen Victoria's yachts, the *Elfin*. Built in 1849 and of a diminutive 98 tons, she acquired the nickname 'The Queen's Messenger'.

The Queen's yacht *Osborne* took its name from her favourite royal residence at Osborne on the Isle of Wight. The last of the paddle-wheel royal vessels, she was of timber construction and had three masts. *Osborne* made the news in June 1877 when her commanding officer reported to the Admiralty the sighting of an unidentified sea monster off the north coast of Sicily.

The royal yacht *Victoria and Albert*, 1908, is seen as a background to the royal party who appear to be making their way ashore in a steam pinnace; the old Queen has passed on and her son, King Edward VII, has taken her place.

The *Victoria and Albert* leaving harbour, 1908, with both the Gosport and Portsmouth shores lined with well-wishers to send the royal party on its way.

ENTENTE CORDIALE

The *entente cordiale* between Great Britain and France marked 1905 as an important year in Anglo-French relations. During August the French Northern Squadron visited Portsmouth with six battleships and twelve additional warships. Crowds lined the shores and harbour vantage points to welcome the ships and their crews.

The entrance to HM Gunwharf was lavishly decorated with 'Welcome', and '1905' illuminated with electric lighting.

Matelots, in a friendly invasion, congregate in
the town hall square.

Sporting events were organized between sailors of both nations, tramcars taking them to the recreation
ground at North End.

The corporation contributed to the festivities by illuminating the leading tram in the procession.

The same vehicle is viewed from its other side.

A particularly novel way of welcoming their guests was displayed at HMS *Excellent*, Whale Island, when men of the Royal Navy formed up to spell out, *Vive la France*.

The principal streets and shopping areas were also decorated as a welcome to the visiting French sailors; Palmerston Road is such an example.

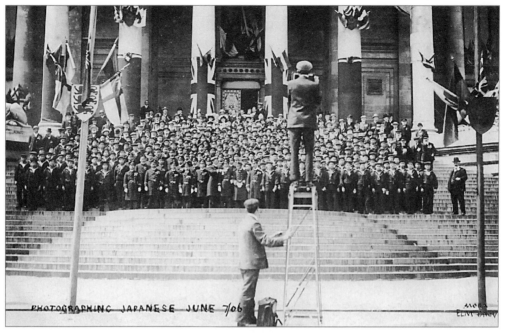

In June 1906, and again in July 1907, representative vessels of the Imperial Japanese Navy visited Portsmouth. They, like the French, were afforded a civic welcome. A pictorial reminder of the 1906 occasion is being recorded, somewhat precariously, by a photographer at the foot of the town hall steps.

As with the earlier French visit, Japanese sailors toured the town in decorated tramcars and are seen here at the junction of London Road with Kingston Crescent.

NAVAL & MILITARY
IMPRESSIONS

Facilities for entertainment within the new Royal Navy barracks, opened in 1903, included, surprisingly, the bandstand pictured here. It is not known when or why it was removed – local folk, today, have no recollection of its being there. The sailors' canteen is the building on the left.

Prior to quarters being provided for them in the new barracks, sailors had been accommodated in old sailing hulks in the dockyard and harbour. The luxury of a shore-based galley must have been a welcome addition to a previously primitive life style.

ROYAL NAVY N° 26.

JACK LEARNING TO SWIM
WITH HIS CLOTHES ON.

The new Royal Navy pool, 1905. The ability to swim was not a necessary requirement for those wishing to join the Navy . . . one could always be taught later!

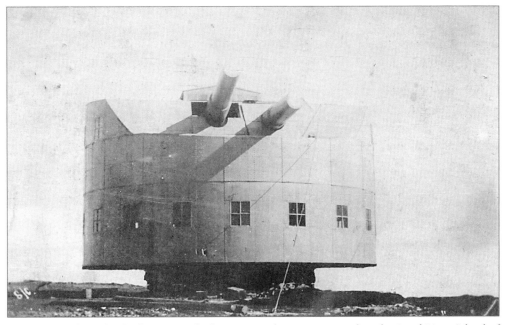

A full-size replica of a ship's turret, a barbette, existed as a training aid at the Royal Navy School of Gunnery at HMS *Excellent*, Whale Island. A similar feature of naval gunnery practice was also to be found at the Royal Marine ranges at Eastney.

A recent ministerial announcement that, owing to constraints upon both manpower and finances, the traditional annual field gun competition is unlikely to continue into the future, has been met with disbelief and disappointment by both service personnel and civilians alike. Reflecting upon happier, and perhaps more stable times, the winning team representing HMS *Excellent* in 1923 is seen here.

Attendance at church parade was compulsory in HM forces until about 1946. This of course resulted in spectacular displays in the numbers of troops on parade. The 6th Hants Regiment is seen marching through High Street, Old Portsmouth heading, it would appear, for the church of St Thomas.

6 June 1912 was obviously a very special day for members of the 6th Hants Regiment for, following the church parade in Old Portsmouth, they were provided with lunch at a local drill hall.

During the First World War, Branksmere, the Southsea home of the Brickwood family, was made available as a Red Cross hospital. At a garden fête and bazaar held in the grounds in July 1917, convalescent patients fraternize with the nursing staff.

Patients and lady visitors enjoy fishing for fun in the ornamental pool.

Royal Marines are synonymous with Portsmouth; the proud association of the city with the corps is one which can be traced to at least 1755 when the marines were raised as a permanent corps under Admiralty control. The picture is of the main gate of the barracks at Eastney, *c.* 1910.

The Church of St Andrew at Eastney, affectionately known as the 'crinoline church', served as a place of worship for the marines until 1905 when a larger, purpose-built St Andrew's was opened in Henderson Road.

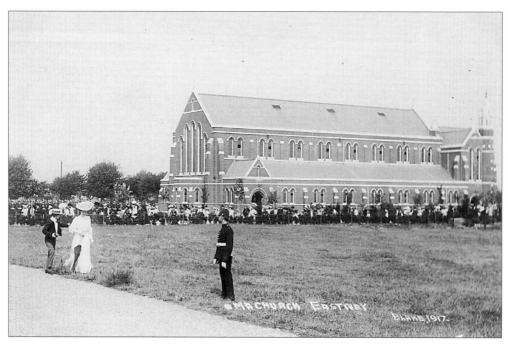

The new St Andrew's is pictured following a Sunday church parade in 1910.

Eastney barracks housed its full complement of marines by 1867. The facilities provided to cater for many hundreds of men were the most modern of the day; witness the cookhouse, c. 1910.

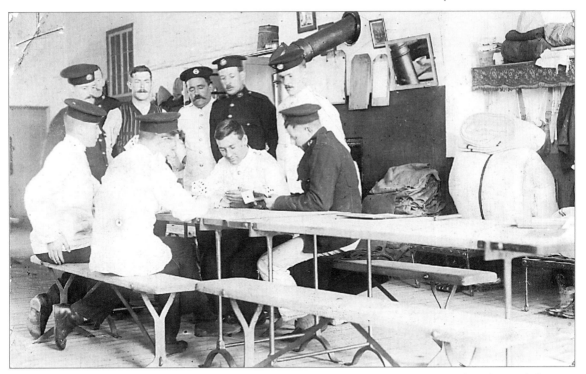

Food prepared in the cookhouse was consumed in the various messes. The tables, when cleared, provided a leisure area for those men who were off duty. A card game excites considerable interest.

Fort Cumberland and its gunnery ranges were the training grounds for men of the Royal Marine Artillery.

At Fort Cumberland, marines are relaxing during 'stand easy', the equivalent of the soldier's NAAFI break. The photograph is captioned 'Active & Passive'.

Men of No. 3 Squadron RMA find time to enjoy a smoke and a bite to eat during a working break.

'All work and no play'. The gymnasium, in addition to providing a regular physical training programme, also became a further leisure facility for those off duty fitness 'freaks'. On this occasion children, probably of serving members, are being introduced to the apparatus.

Sited outside Southsea Castle, the Battery House provided gunnery training for marine artillerymen, simulating conditions under which they would serve at sea. It was in use by them from 1848 until they moved to Fort Cumberland in 1859.

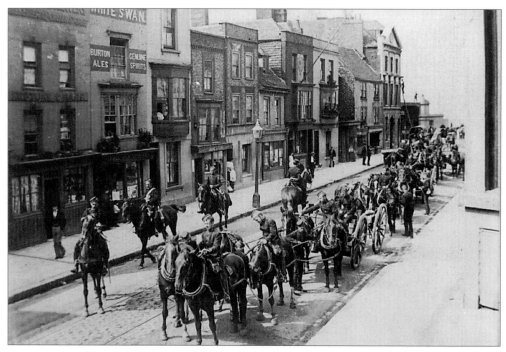

These two photographs feature teams of Royal Marine Artillerymen with horses, field guns and limbers in Broad Street, Old Portsmouth, 28 August 1894.

Returning from combined exercises on the Browndown Ranges at Gosport, they have just disembarked from the chain ferry which has brought them across the harbour.

Recreation facilities were provided in the canteen building.

Senior ranks enjoyed the home comforts of the sergeants' mess.

All ranks were encouraged to avail themselves of the facilities provided at the library and reading room.

The building on the left of the picture was, and still is, known as 'Teapot Row'. Built as quarters for the field officers in 1866, it has now passed into civilian hands following the sale of barrack properties. The unusual name, of which the origin is not known, is still applied to the private dwellings now occupying the block.

EDUCATION

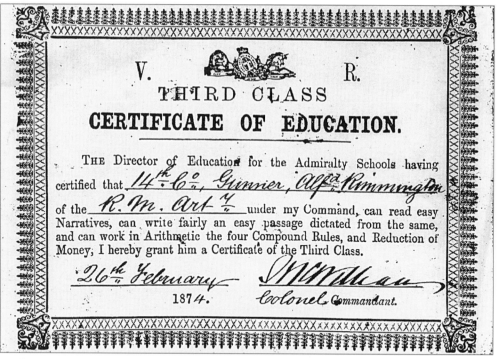

Briefly remaining with the Royal Marines, this Certificate of Education, Third Class, was awarded to Gunner Alfred Rimmington in 1874. Education was provided for all ranks, should they wish to further their careers, at a school within the barracks itself.

A number of local churches provided Sunday and day schools for children of parishioners; Lake Road Baptist church was probably the largest. A photograph taken in June 1913 reveals a surprisingly large teaching staff.

One of the most successful local church-sponsored schools was the day school of the Circus Church in Surrey Street. The following four pictures are a selection of a number purchased at a local charity auction in 1988. The girl displays a slate bearing the legend 'Standard V'.

Circus Church girls' 11. The Circus Church originated in a redundant equestrian circus building and later moved to purpose-built church and school premises in Surrey Street.

Circus School, Portsmouth, group 12. The move into the new church premises took place on 28 December 1864 and, although it has not been possible to date these photographs, they appear to have been taken within the first ten years of this century.

Circus School, Portsmouth, group 13. Obviously taken over a number of years, the pictures seem to follow a possible, annual sequence; a study of the childish faces show several of the girls to be, albeit a little older, in more than one study.

Non-academic pursuits include the production of school plays and here, in 1913, the cast of *The Good Natured Man* stage such a drama at the boys' secondary school in Southsea. Left to right are: H.C. Pottle, W.H. Thomas, C.H. Churchill, A.G. Tucker and S.J. Fielder. The school roll of honour of those old boys who lost their lives in the First World War includes C.H. Churchill.

Sporting interests have long been part of the school curriculum, and at Solent Road in Farlington the girl's netball team is pictured, *c*. 1927.

While girls have traditionally played netball, boys indulged in the game of football. Winners of the School's Cup in the 1938–9 season, the Wimborne Road School team proudly pose for this group photograph, their captain, 'Dickie' Moore, occupying centre stage.

The closure of our schools at the start of the Second World War meant that children who were not evacuated were deprived of education. Schemes introduced to overcome this unforeseen problem involved opening temporary centres of learning on a part-time basis. The children pictured here are receiving tuition at the Farlington Church of the Resurrection.

One of just a few old buildings to survive in Portsea is the Beneficial School, endowed as a charitable foundation in 1784. With the surrounding area now cleared of properties destroyed by bomb damage, the building stands alone with a landscaped approach made possible by that clearance.

Continuing in an educational role, the Beneficial School is now a work experience centre providing training for young people in a variety of trades.

Apparently starting life as St Nicholas's Mission Hall, the Buckland Academy, seen here in about 1906, later became the Magdala Academy. Many varied claims of instruction to high educational standards were made as shown by the window advertisements. The Christian Spiritualist Church seems to have occupied the building at a later date.

It is hoped that readers can perhaps help to identify the origins of the building seen here, 1969. It was the premises of a wholesale meat distributor, but had earlier been the location of Laws' School for Boys. Nothing is known of this educational establishment and local directories offer no clue. The two-storey property of substantial proportions was sited in Greetham Street and no longer exists.

Drayton Road school at North End was the first school casualty of the Second World War when it was struck by a German bomb during an early evening raid on Portsmouth, 11 July 1940. The city's first civilian deaths due to bombing were also sustained here when first aid workers on duty at the school were killed.

SOUTHSEA

Clarence Pier, originally constructed in 1842 for the Isle of Wight steamer trade, was enlarged and improved in June 1861 and became a mecca of entertainment in the fast growing resort of Southsea. The pier and its pavilion were destroyed by enemy bombing during the Second World War.

Given fine weather, the attractions of seaside piers were numerous; band concerts were given, alfresco, by the regimental units based in Portsmouth, while Sunday and evening performances of light entertainment and choral works were enjoyed within the pavilion. Above all the pier deck provided a leisure area where promenading could be enjoyed by all.

The pier, *c.* 1895, seen under conditions not in any way favourable for a sea trip. A steamer is approaching after a cold crossing from the island. Note the ice along the shoreline.

Clarence Pier and the Esplanade Hotel are to the left of this picture, *c.* 1896. Circus animals, elephants and camels are featured with the big top sited in an adjacent field.

3   SOUTHSEA. — On the Esplanade. — LL.

Sunday fashions were worn by both ladies and gents on their excursions to the seaside. However hot and cumbersome their clothing, pride took precedence over comfort. The pier and hotel form the background.

SOUTHSEA BEACH.

During the season, market traders took advantage of the numbers who visited the beach to sell their wares. Stalls were commonly set up on the shoreline itself.

In a picture postcard of 1906, we may see that Clarence beach was the place to be at 5 p.m. on August bank holiday. The numbers visiting the promenade, beach and common are astonishing!

Portsmouth Swimming Club once claimed that its membership was greater than any other, worldwide. By 1903, the date of this photograph, sea bathing was no longer frowned upon if conducted with discretion and decorum. Following these rules, the club made a considerable investment to provide a suitable site and facilities for its members.

Behind the club building were covered bathing pontoons. Male and female bathers are seen at a discreet distance from one another.

A byelaw of 1877 ordered that the regulation bathing dress was to be a garment, or combination of garments, extending from the neck to the knees and to be of a thickness, material and shape sufficiently effective to prevent indecent exposure of the bather.

Entry into the water was negotiated via the steps which at low tide were at some height above the beach. Not a venture for the faint-hearted!

Eastney beach catered for individuals, or perhaps family groups, who would hire the bathing machines seen here in 1909.

Still a popular walk in this present age, the Ladies' Mile was a favourite spot to promenade in your 'best and newest frock', and to be seen in competition with others in equally fine attire.

Holiday-makers were attracted to Southsea with hotels such as the Royal Pier. Regrettably this very fine building from about 1880 was demolished in late 1995, in favour of a proposed university hall of

Visitors and native Portsmuthians alike were drawn to the attractions of Southsea's main shopping areas. King's Road was one such venue until it was razed to the ground during air raids.

Elm Grove, once entirely tree lined, was also a prime shopping centre and, as a continuation of King's Road, presented the serious shopper with one mile of quality shops.

Possibly the finest of Southsea's shops were located in Palmerston Road and, sad to say, they also suffered total annihilation in the blitz on Portsmouth.

Castle Buildings, Southsea, where tea and tourist information could be obtained. Sited near Southsea Castle and opposite the bandstand and skating rink, Portsmouth's Entertainments, Publicity and Trading Offices were also housed in the building.

The popularity of the bandstand faded when military bands were otherwise engaged for the duration of the war. There had been upwards of six such venues for public entertainment in the city; most with a surrounding dance and skating area. This, the only surviving example, is now converted for use as a skate park.

Southsea Miniature Railway, 1937; this proved to be a great attraction both before and after the war years.

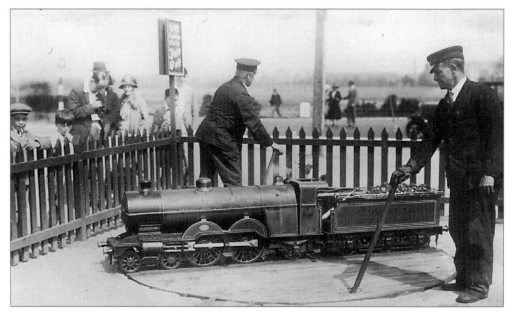

Returning to the station, the locomotive was placed on the turntable to reverse its direction in readiness for the next trip.

The train leaving platform one. It carries its passengers on a circular journey around the children's pool and play area.

Without question, the most popular and enduring jewel in Southsea's crown has been its pier. The first South Parade Pier, seen here, was privately owned and opened in July 1879.

Tragedy struck in 1904 when, on 19 July, fire destroyed the pavilion building and much of the timber construction.

Wisely the corporation decided to purchase the derelict remains and rebuild on a grander scale.

The finishing touches are being applied to the new South Parade Pier which, at a cost of £70,000, reopened to the public on 12 August 1908.

BAND STAND & SKATING RINK, SOUTH PARADE PIER SOUTHSEA.

Many additional attractions were introduced including a skating rink, reading room and the ubiquitous bandstand.

The Pavilion, South Parade Pier, Southsea

The pavilion theatre provided a venue for summer shows, plays, orchestral and band concerts; dancing was catered for with two ballrooms and two bands.

The pier suffered a disastrous set-back when in 1974, during the filming of the rock musical *Tommy*, fire completely destroyed the theatre and dance halls.

Rising, phoenix-like, from the ashes for the second time, the pier, with a modified silhouette, was rebuilt at a cost of £600,000 and opened in time for the summer season, 1975.

INDUSTRY

Trade directories published during this century show a continuous and expected decline in the number of blacksmiths, general smiths and farriers practising their craft within the city. Possibly the last of these were the premises of Maurice Ablitt & Sons in Nancy Road, Fratton, photographed in 1979.

Shortly before the outbreak of the Second World War, there had been eleven independent foundries in Portsmouth; that number had been reduced to just one, Sperring's Albion Iron Works, before the final closure of that company in 1973, when the foundry and adjacent lands were acquired for development by the City Council.

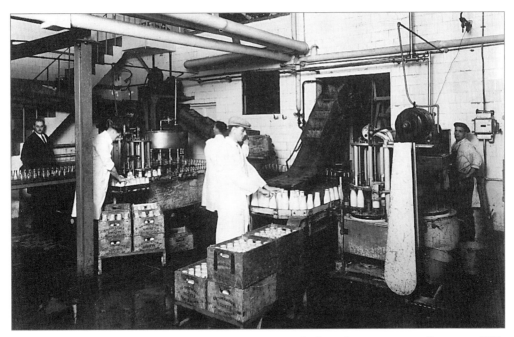

The move by Portsea Island Co-operative Dairies to purpose-built modern premises in Copnor, *c.* 1930, placed the company ahead of their rivals in the town. New, improved production methods enabled the daily output to be substantially increased, Ernest Ricketts, snr, is centre stage at the conveyor line while supervisor, Mr Jolliff, far left, watches.

Sporting competition between Co-op departments was encouraged among the staff, the dairy gaining its fair share of trophies. Pictured is the winning tug of war team in 1933. Ernest Ricketts is again pictured, second left, back row.

Co-operative Dairy roundsmen pause briefly to pose for this informal study, *c*. 1930.

The Southsea Dairy Company show their might at the headquarters building in Marmion Road. In the first decade of this century the firm was the largest in the town, having fifteen branches. Before the introduction of bottles and cartons, milk was delivered from large churns carried on the carts.

Sailing barges in Langstone harbour, carrying their loads of shingle to bases at both Milton and Langstone village.

The extraction of shingle from banks off the Hayling shore and entrance to Langstone harbour has been a local industry for generations. In the early years sailing barges were beached at low tide, shingle dug by spade straight into the hold, the barges refloated at high water and the cargo taken ashore to be unloaded.

The company of Charles Samuel Kendall began trading in aggregates from a small wharf site in Velder Lake in 1916. In the early years, sand and gravel was extracted by hand, with only the aid of shovels and wheelbarrows. At the wharf a small steam crane would unload the material, which was then taken away by horse and cart. Mr Kendall is seen, standing, wearing a pale-coloured cap.

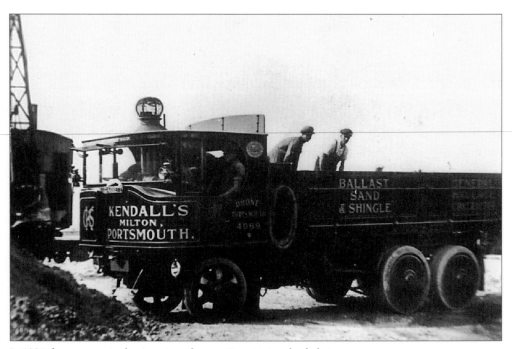

In 1931 the company took possession of a new Garrett six-wheeled steam wagon.

The vehicle demonstrates its capabilities.

The steam dredger SS *Graball*, and vessels of her type, had long ago replaced the sailing barges which, for the most part, now lay rotting in the creeks and rythes of Portsmouth and Hayling. The *Graball* carried about 350 tons of ballast and was loaded by jib and crane.

Constructing the 'Gateway to Europe', Portsmouth's Continental ferry port, on 10 acres of tidal mudland, involved the removal by dredging, of thousands of cubic yards of silt, mud and debris from the Rudmore shoreline.

Reclamation of the mudlands completed, the building of the port could begin; docking facilities, customs and terminal buildings, car and lorry parks. Portsmouth's Continental ferry port was finally declared open for business on 16 June 1976, exactly one year after work commenced.

PANORAMA
AND POSTSCRIPT

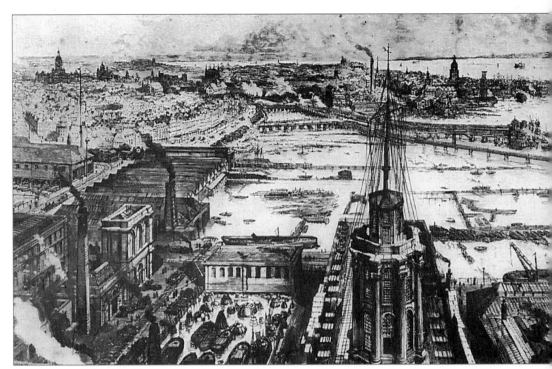

Issued free with the *Graphic* newspaper, *c.* 1898, the panorama is an important, illustrative source of local history. Details too numerous to mention are included in this engraving by H.W. Brewer; it remains for the reader to study and discover the very many features of Victorian Portsmouth, Gosport and the harbour. The semaphore tower was destroyed by fire in 1913. It has been suggested that preliminary sketches of the entire panorama were made while the artist was high above the scene in a tethered balloon. The original copy is displayed in the old Wymering manor house, Cosham.

The Gaiety Cinema pictured on the right, faces Highland Road school. The road bridge, beneath which ran the East Southsea Railway, is seen between the two buildings.

The East Southsea branch line from Fratton was closed at the outbreak of war in 1914, never to reopen. It was not until 1926, however, that the rails were removed and the land developed for housing. Highland Road railway bridge is seen in the distance.

Continuing with the theme of East Southsea. The seashore fronting HMS *St George* (Fraser Battery) is still littered with the remains of anti-tank blocks, a reminder of the defensive line which was placed around our coasts to repel and deter enemy invasion forces.

Eastney police station, the smallest of those in our local force, and sited on the corner of Essex and Eastney Roads, was considered, by serving officers, to be the 'home from home' among police stations. A police ambulance was originally garaged in the building at the rear. The building has now been demolished, and the site remains vacant.

Children gather in Methuen Road, Eastney, *c.* 1912. For most of them this will be their first appearance before a camera.

An unusual subject for a photograph, Morely Road is seen separated from Highland Street by a wall. It is said that this barrier was erected to stop 'those vulgar working class residents from Highland Street from infiltrating Morley Road'. Whatever the real reason, the corporation finally removed the offending wall in 1976 at a cost of £2,200.

The few items remaining in this volume are advertisements designed to jolt the memories of older readers, and provide younger people with descriptions and prices of goods and services available in 'the good old days'. The Edison Phonograph of 1904, advertised at 4s 6d, would sell today, at auction, for perhaps £75.

The only regular means of 'flying' from Portsmouth to the Isle of Wight in this present age is to travel by hovercraft at a fare exceeding £6 return; compare this then with an advertisement of 1937 when a day return to Ryde by air was as little as 5s 6d.

Royal Pier Hotel,
——SOUTHSEA——

Manageress - Miss BRAINE.

This Hotel has been recently re-decorated, re-furnished, and re-fitted with every modern appliance calculated to ensure the comfort of individual guests, families, naval and military officers, and the highest nobility.

The Cuisine and Cellars are equal to the tastes of the epicure and the valetudinarian. Splendid views are obtained of the Military Manoeuvres on Southsea Common, the Yachting on the Solent, the Anchorage at Spithead, and over the shores of the Isle of Wight.

MODERATE TARIFF.

The reader is referred to p. 100. The grandeur of the building exactly matches the extravagant claims of the manageress, Miss Braine, in an advertisement of 1904.

Portsmouth Park Racecourse

Situated in a picturesque spot at the foot of Portsdown Hill on the Southampton Road. The racecourse is leased for a number of years to Northolt Park Ltd., the proprietors of the famous course in London, the amenities of which rival those of any racecourse in England.

The Racing is conducted under the Rules of the Pony Turf Club.

The transport facilities to and from the course are unique, as Paulsgrove Halt Station is situated right on the course and the Southern Railway run a most efficient service of cheap excursions on race days. There are also ample Southdown 'buses which serve the racecourse from nearby districts.

The race meetings are fully advertised in the local papers, and any enquiries can be made of local Secretary : Mr. F. W. Ward, 17, Landport Terrace, Portsmouth.

List of Fixtures for 1937 Season

Monday (B.H.)	Mar. 29th	Monday (B.H.)	Aug. 2nd
Saturday	May 8th	Wednesday	Aug. 18th
Wednesday	May 26th	Saturday	Sept. 11th
Saturday	July 3rd	Saturday	Oct. 9th
Wednesday	July 14th	Saturday	Oct. 30th

Portsmouth Park Racecourse at Paulsgrove was the second such enterprise to bear the title; the first had its origins in Farlington where, in 1891, the Portsmouth Park Club was established. The entire undertaking was taken over by the War Office in 1915. The Paulsgrove course opened in 1928 for pony racing and was closed at the outbreak of war in 1939.

The Highbury housing estate was established in Cosham in the mid-1930s. With fitted, 'luxury' kitchens and bathrooms and planned front gardens, these properties were then the ultimate in modern housing. Dream homes at affordable prices, they could be purchased for as little as £25 deposit and a minimum repayment of 21s 11d per week!

ACKNOWLEDGEMENTS

The successful completion of this book would not have been possible without the help of many kind friends and colleagues, organizations and institutions who have given advice and information and permitted the reproduction of photographs from their own collections.

My friendly working relationship with the city museums and records office is a long-standing one and I am indebted to Sarah Quail and her staff who have been particularly generous in allowing me access to the city's photographic archives.

Thanks are also due to the photographic department of Portsmouth University and the *News Portsmouth*, whose files of the earlier *Evening News* and *Hampshire Telegraph* are a never-ending and valuable source of information to local historians.

In addition, my sincere appreciation is offered to the Nature Conservancy, Solent Road School PTA, Kendall Brothers of Portsmouth, Cynthia Shaw, Sue Krisman, Eric Rimmington, Peter Barge, Arthur Ricketts, David Jordan, David Francis, Christopher Collins, Mrs B. Reeves, Mrs E. Hedley, Mr K. Biles, Mr A. Jones and the late Bill Buckley.

As with any acknowledged sources, it is always possible that reference to a particular item or individual has been omitted; my apologies are extended for any such imprudence should it have occurred.

Finally, acknowledgement is given to the very many photographers, living or perhaps now dead, who were responsible for the originals of all the photographs and who recorded those times, places and events for posterity and our enjoyment.

BRITAIN IN OLD PHOTOGRAPHS

Lincoln
Lincoln Cathedral
The Lincolnshire Coast
Liverpool
Around Llandudno
Around Lochaber
Theatrical London
Around Louth
The Lower Fal Estuary
Lowestoft
Luton
Lympne Airfield
Lytham St Annes
Maidenhead
Around Maidenhead
Around Malvern
Manchester
Manchester Road & Rail
Mansfield
Marlborough: A Second Selection
Marylebone & Paddington
Around Matlock
Melton Mowbray
Around Melksham
The Mendips
Merton & Morden
Middlesbrough
Midsomer Norton & Radstock
Around Mildenhall
Milton Keynes
Minehead
Monmouth & the River Wye
The Nadder Valley
Newark
Around Newark
Newbury
Newport, Isle of Wight
The Norfolk Broads
Norfolk at War
North Fylde
North Lambeth
North Walsham & District
Northallerton
Northampton
Around Norwich
Nottingham 1944–74
The Changing Face of Nottingham
Victorian Nottingham
Nottingham Yesterday & Today
Nuneaton
Around Oakham
Ormskirk & District
Otley & District
Oxford: The University
Oxford Yesterday & Today
Oxfordshire Railways: A Second
    Selection
Oxfordshire at School
Around Padstow
Pattingham & Wombourne

Penwith
Penzance & Newlyn
Around Pershore
Around Plymouth
Poole
Portsmouth
Poulton-le-Fylde
Preston
Prestwich
Pudsey
Radcliffe
RAF Chivenor
RAF Cosford
RAF Hawkinge
RAF Manston
RAF Manston: A Second Selection
RAF St Mawgan
RAF Tangmere
Ramsgate & Thanet Life
Reading
Reading: A Second Selection
Redditch & the Needle District
Redditch: A Second Selection
Richmond, Surrey
Rickmansworth
Around Ripley
The River Soar
Romney Marsh
Romney Marsh: A Second
    Selection
Rossendale
Around Rotherham
Rugby
Around Rugeley
Ruislip
Around Ryde
St Albans
St Andrews
Salford
Salisbury
Salisbury: A Second Selection
Salisbury: A Third Selection
Around Salisbury
Sandhurst & Crowthorne
Sandown & Shanklin
Sandwich
Scarborough
Scunthorpe
Seaton, Lyme Regis & Axminster
Around Seaton & Sidmouth
Sedgley & District
The Severn Vale
Sherwood Forest
Shrewsbury
Shrewsbury: A Second Selection
Shropshire Railways
Skegness
Around Skegness
Skipton & the Dales
Around Slough

Smethwick
Somerton & Langport
Southampton
Southend-on-Sea
Southport
Southwark
Southwell
Southwold to Aldeburgh
Stafford
Around Stafford
Staffordshire Railways
Around Staveley
Stepney
Stevenage
The History of Stilton Cheese
Stoke-on-Trent
Stoke Newington
Stonehouse to Painswick
Around Stony Stratford
Around Stony Stratford: A Second
    Selection
Stowmarket
Streatham
Stroud & the Five Valleys
Stroud & the Five Valleys: A
    Second Selection
Stroud's Golden Valley
The Stroudwater and Thames &
    Severn Canals
The Stroudwater and Thames &
    Severn Canals: A Second
    Selection
Suffolk at Work
Suffolk at Work: A Second
    Selection
The Heart of Suffolk
Sunderland
Sutton
Swansea
Swindon: A Third Selection
Swindon: A Fifth Selection
Around Tamworth
Taunton
Around Taunton
Teesdale
Teesdale: A Second Selection
Tenbury Wells
Around Tettenhall & Codshall
Tewkesbury & the Vale of
    Gloucester
Thame to Watlington
Around Thatcham
Around Thirsk
Thornbury to Berkeley
Tipton
Around Tonbridge
Trowbridge
Around Truro
TT Races
Tunbridge Wells

Tunbridge Wells: A Second
    Selection
Twickenham
Uley, Dursley & Cam
The Upper Fal
The Upper Tywi Valley
Uxbridge, Hillingdon & Cowley
The Vale of Belvoir
The Vale of Conway
Ventnor
Wakefield
Wallingford
Walsall
Waltham Abbey
Wandsworth at War
Wantage, Faringdon & the Vale
    Villages
Around Warwick
Weardale
Weardale: A Second Selection
Wednesbury
Wells
Welshpool
West Bromwich
West Wight
Weston-super-Mare
Around Weston-super-Mare
Weymouth & Portland
Around Wheatley
Around Whetstone
Whitchurch to Market Drayton
Around Whitstable
Wigton & the Solway Plain
Willesden
Around Wilton
Wimbledon
Around Windsor
Wingham, Addisham &
    Littlebourne
Wisbech
Witham & District
Witney
Around Witney
The Witney District
Wokingham
Around Woodbridge
Around Woodstock
Woolwich
Woolwich Royal Arsenal
Around Wootton Bassett,
    Cricklade & Purton
Worcester
Worcester in a Day
Around Worcester
Worcestershire at Work
Around Worthing
Wotton-under-Edge to Chipping
    Sodbury
Wymondham & Attleborough
The Yorkshire Wolds

To order any of these titles please telephone our distributor, Littlehampton Book Services on 01903 721596
For a catalogue of these and our other titles please ring Regina Schinner on 01453 731114